BE YOUR OWN BOSS: YOU CAN DO IT

BY NADIA SAHARI

DISCLAIMER

Nothing in this life is guaranteed or a sure thing when it comes to what we do or say. Knowledge is given to us by reading books, by listening to media, by life experience in general. But we need to be sure that what we listen to and what we read is positive and good for us. We can apply some things to our lives and others we cannot. If you fail in the beginning once or twice, keep trying and you will succeed. Never give up.

I want you to know this is just a guide. I am not claiming this is a know it all and get rich quick guide. I am giving you something to start with, a tool to help you get started, to answer some questions you may have. By no means am I saying that this a sure guaranteed way for you to be successful or to get rich. I am sharing with you ideas from my own experiences and successes.

Where you go with this guide is all up to you. Your dream, your passion and persistence will get you where you want to be. You can do it if I can. You are a superstar.

Address inquiries to:

Venus Moon Press
5401 FM 1626
Ste. 170-177
Kyle, TX 78640

https://www.venusmoonpress.com

Library of Congress Cataloging-in-Publication Data

Sahari, Nadia [date]

Be Your Own Boss: You Can Do It

ISBN 978-1-938140-21-1

Library of Congress Control Number 2012934974

Nadia Sahari [date] 2. Business 3. Entrepreneurship 4. Self-help 5. Biography 6. Motivational, 7. Inspirational 8. Friends 9. Webinars 10. Courses 11. Websites 12. Success 13. Faith,14. Believe 15. Passion

Table of Contents

DISCLAIMER 2
     Chapter 1 7
My Credentials 7
     Chapter 2 18
What Is Your Dream? 18
     Chapter 3 21
How to be Legal at a Low Cost....................................21
     Chapter 4 25
Equipping Your Store..25
     Chapter 5 28
How to Find Manufacturers 28
     Chapter 6 30
Your Greatest Resource 30
     Chapter 7 33
Do You Need Investors? 33
Passion + Patience + Persistence = Success................34
     Chapter 8 36
Ideas For Startups...36
     Chapter 9 39
Who's The Boss? 39
     Chapter 10 42
Marketing 42
     Chapter 11 45
Forgotten Adventure 45
     Chapter 12 48
The Studio 48

Chapter 13 51

Online Courses 51

Chapter 14 54

Assistance for Anything Business 54

Chapter 15 57

Networking! 57

Chapter 16 60

Platforms; Best Live Streaming! 60

Chapter 17 64

Email List To Market Your Business/Products 64

Chapter 18 67

My Life Today 67

Chapter19 70

Step by Step Guide 70

Chapter 20 73

Resources..73

Chapter 1

My Credentials

I have been an entrepreneur for over thirty years. I believe you should know a little about the businesses I began, how and why I did it. I started my first business venture at the age of twenty-five. I only had three hundred dollars to start my idea and business venture. I had no education in business, never owned one, always punched a time clock. I got tired of the jobs and only lasted about three months at each one. I got bored with the monotony of the tasks. I quit each one for that reason as well as being sexually harassed by my male employers.

I was so fed up with it all, but I needed to work because I had two little children at the time to worry about. So, I took the risk. I was willing to try anything to be successful at something.

I wanted to buy a house for my children to grow up in and I knew that my husband at that time (I'm now married to someone else) would never be able to do that for my children and me. He had child support to pay and worked hard for a meat packing company for pennies. In his younger years he was a very famous drummer and performed with many of the super stars like Ritchie Valens, Buddy Holly, Big Bopper, Fabian, Paul Anka, Connie Francis, Shelly Fabre, and many more. Most of his paycheck went to his ex-wife. So, I had to be creative and start my own business to get what I wanted. I had never owned a business; I did not know a thing about what to do or how to start. I knew this: Don't take handouts. Do it yourself. Don't expect others to do it for you. Take responsibility for your own life, this will make you successful.

I did it all with passion. I had plenty of passion to be free from stress and finances. I wanted to make a lot of money, that was my goal. Money would set me free from punching a clock and waiting a hundred years to own a house if I depended on my husband to do it.

The first thing I did was to create an idea. I asked myself

what to do. I had my best friend Jenny to bounce ideas off. She loved my idea. She asked me things; we both had the same taste in clothes and most things. What do I love more than anything and cannot afford to buy much of? What would women and men love to have? I repeatedly asked myself questions. I thought of several things, and suddenly what came to mind was lingerie. Yes, beautiful, sexy, unique pieces of lingerie not found in any other store. (I was ahead of my time; now there are plenty of stores doing this.) I told Jenny, she was ecstatic.

What should I call the store? How to attract both and women? I pondered for a day or two. When driving my sons to school I asked them what ideas they had to name my business. They were incredible. Without hesitation they both yelled at the same time: Foxee' Lady*!* Geniuses! They took the name from Jimi Hendrix's song Foxy Lady. I loved it! I modified it to make it look French and to give it a flair. I spelled it Foxee' Lady. That was the beginning.

I asked a friend who worked at a bank what I had to do to register the business name and protect myself. She told me I needed to register it at the County Clerk's office. I drove to Detroit and arrived at the County Clerk's office, filled out the fictitious name form and paid something like ten dollars. It was very inexpensive. That is the first thing I did after choosing a name for the business. Then I went back to the bank with the documents from the County Clerk and opened an account for Foxee' Lady.

Next, I looked for a space to lease to open my lingerie store as soon as possible. I searched in my hometown of Troy and in a town nearby. I found a new building in Rochester Hills, Michigan, about an hour from Detroit. I called the number on the sign for leasing info and set up an appointment to meet with the owner. I believe that is the town where Madonna grew up. It was before she left for New York and became famous. She may have come into my boutique at some point—who knows? I met with the owner, Tony, and he gave me a guided tour of all the available spaces. There were about ten spaces, five on each side and one at the end of the building that was a Greek restaurant. I selected the one that I wanted and could afford. It was only three hundred square feet. I signed the lease for two years.

There were only three of us in The Little Mall—the other

seven spaces had not been rented yet. A cute young man with long hair and jeans operated a leather shop. Len was a hippie a very cool and very nice guy. He was also very talented and made leather belts and wallets by hand. A young Greek man named Demetrius owned the Greek restaurant. He made delicious Souvlaki. I met both young men and we instantly became friends and supported each other in our business ventures. I knew it was going to be fun to be in business.

The closer opening day came, the more fun I had. It was a rush like I had never felt before. Going one step at a time, I moved in racks, hangers, etc. My best friend's Italian husband Vincent was a carpenter, the best and still is today. He built my counter for me. I called the phone company and set up my phone service. I bought a cash register, tape, two sales books from an office supply, pencils, pens, stapler and all the tools I needed. No one told me what to do or where to go for things I needed. I naturally knew what I should do and what not to do. It was like eating candy.

Through research (no internet then) I learned that Chicago was going to have a convention for retailers. I registered to go to the convention to make connections I needed to run my business. I took my best friend with me. Jenny was so excited she could not wait to go. We drove to Chicago, only about four hours away from the Detroit area, and attended the show. I made connections for my lingerie orders. I only ordered what I knew I would get within a week. I wanted to open the store without delay. I was excited to be at the show, but after the second day of walking the convention, I was ready to go home. The second day was very hard. Everything seemed to look the same. I could not continue the buying trip. Two days at a convention is still max for me.

I had my sources, and I was happy. I bought what I would wear myself. Jenny and I both bought clothing for ourselves. What a shopping trip!

Back in Rochester Hills, I did what I had to do to get things ready for my grand opening. I was all set up. I even hired a CPA to handle my receipts and taxes. I couldn't afford a CPA, but I had this idea in my head that I was going to make a lot of money. I was ready. One week later the packages began to arrive. I could only fill one wall on one side with lingerie. As the lingerie came in, I priced each item and hung them all up. While I was doing this, customers from the restaurant and leather shop came in. They were curious. One by one all my lingerie items were sold before I even opened the shop! Now, I had a thousand dollars for inventory.

I called the manufacturer and placed an order for the whole thousand. I doubled my order in one day. I was really excited now. I had something different and unique. I had something that women and men wanted lingerie. My lingerie was classy, sexy, beautiful, and very feminine things that you could not find anywhere. I was ecstatic. A week later I received my shipment and had more items than the week before. A thousand dollars purchased a lot of items. In less than two weeks I sold all the lingerie and this time I tripled my sales. I now had three thousand dollars.

I raised my prices having realized I had sold the first shipment too cheaply. My prices were fabulous even tripled. Nobody had this kind of lingerie. I ordered more items: garter belts, sexy panties, sexy bras, nightgowns, teddys and more. Jenny loved all my stuff. We picked out our favorites and took them home.

I opened with the store fully stocked, thanks to all the customers who helped me out before the official opening. My friends and neighbors at the mall, Len, and Demetrius, were very supportive and in awe of what was happening. I advertised on the radio. The male voiceover and sexy mood music in the background were perfect to attract lawyers, doctors, homemakers, secretaries, and anyone who wanted something different and sexy.

Business was booming so I had to hire help. I hired a young girl to help me since I had two children to get home to each evening and they had games after school that I took them to and stayed to watch. When you have children, you have all the games, transportation to and from school, etc. My children were and still are my priority. Of course, my present husband is priority too.

This is an example how I started my life as an entrepreneur and went on from there to be very successful. After the Foxee' Lady store, I opened a second store called Main Street Jeans, to the urging of my landlord at the mall, he was fascinated by my energy, my passion, he wanted me to be his partner in any venture I wanted, so, I picked Jeans, and I named it Main Street Jeans. Tony loved it and provided all the money for me to buy the merchandise. In that store I sold only jeans from Jordache, Guess, Lee, etc. It turned out to be a great store. Sales for both stores skyrocketed. To bring me more income from the two stores, I went to businesses like restaurants and Lounges. I pitched fashion shows with lingerie and fashion Jeans, the owners loved the idea. I hired models in the neighborhood, I modeled as well, and I narrated all the shows that were held during business luncheons. The lunch crowd consisted of executives' men and women, The word spread, and the venues were busier than ever. It was so great, and all the garments were sold on the premises. That is how I paid the models and sold my merchandise. My hours were early morning after I drove my two sons to school, and lasted until three o'clock, when it was time to pick up my sons from school, make dinner, shower, rest awhile and be with my family until I kissed my son's good night around eight at night. My salesclerk took over after that. I wanted to be home for my family. I kept the stores for three years and had to consider selling for health reasons.

During the time I had the stores. I also at the same time starting at nine 'o'clock in the evening, after my sons were sleeping, I performed Belly Dancing with my live band, until two in the morning. At times. I had to do TV talk shows and Telethons, that's when I needed my salesclerk to work and handle the boutique. By the end of the day, and doing all those things, making lots of money too, I was tired. My body couldn't do it all anymore. It was crying for rest. I had to give something up, I had to sell the businesses or die. My doctor advised me to sell or get buried within a six-month period. So, after three years, of retail, fashion shows, belly dancing, teaching, and stresses at home, I sold the businesses.

Soon after that, I moved to Las Vegas. In Las Vegas I worked in cold calling sales on the telephone. Never heard of this job in my life, but I was willing to try. I was going to sell vitamins—the best experience anyone can get. I had no idea what I was doing or if I could do it. I was shy and scared to death of the rejection from all the managers at the pharmacies and health food stores I had to cold call. The company gave me the toughest territory in the USA. That's what they said. It included the New England states, New York, and New Jersey. No one could sell these areas, so they gave them to me. After a couple of months my sales exceeded everyone's.

I became the motivator of the whole company. I could not get sick; I could not call in and not show up. I had to come to work happy to start the day right. If I walked in unhappy, the sales manager grabbed me and walked me into his office. What's wrong? You can't be unhappy."

He would do all he could to make me laugh. I made over eight hundred dollars a week at phone sales working just four hours a day, five days a week. I was ecstatic!

But one day I got the flu and called in to tell my sales manager I could not come to work. He went ballistic. "You must come to work; nobody will sell if you don't come in. Please." I went to work. I was miserable. My sales that day outsold all other salespeople. I was upset that I had to come in so sick. Nobody cared. The vice-president of the company was a tall elderly man and he never smiled. He walked past me smiled and said, "Great job!" Nothing about my fever or how I was feeling. I got up from my cubicle and said goodbye to the other thirty salespeople and left, that was my last day, I decided not to return.

I also thought about all the money I was making for the company and what a small piece of the pie I was getting. I thought of opening my own vitamin company and getting all the pie. So, I did.

My friend, a Lebanese man, encouraged me to do that and he wanted to be my partner. He had no knowledge of Vitamins, I had it all in my head. I was now a single mother, so I needed to do something to earn a living for my sons and me. I agreed. We incorporated, opened an account and business began. We leased a place in a high-rise building called The Atrium in Las Vegas, On Rancho Road. We leased the top floor, and the view was incredible. We bought office furniture and added phone lines and booths for salespeople. I set it up like the company I worked for but a hundred times bigger and better.

My office was in the sales department. We met with labs in California and from there business began. I hired my ex-sales manager and hired most of the salespeople from the previous company I had worked for. It was a rush like you wouldn't believe. I could not wait for the first sale. I had hired all the top salespeople. I hired my secretary who had just moved from New York, a beautiful Italian girl who needed the job badly. Her husband was out of work, Rosie, had two little boys. I hired her on the spot. I contacted VP's and purchasing agents at several grocery store chains to get my product on their shelves. It was a man's world, a young woman VP meeting with these guys was unheard of at the time. Often, I heard that I was very brave to meet with all these execs who were mostly over fifty years old. I was the new kid on the block to them. What gave me the courage to ask them to place my product in their stores? Two words: PASSION & MONEY. I loved being a businesswoman. I loved having my own office and staff. It was an incredible feeling that I will never forget. And Rosie, was the best Secretary anyone could have, and we are best friends today. Just writing this brings all the memories back to me.

What amazed me most is that young girls with bachelor's and master's degrees came to me, a high school dropout, asking to work in my company. I felt so sad for them. They could not find jobs in their field. They wanted any job I may have had. They asked me how I learned the process of opening my own business. I told them it was just an instinct for me and a great passion to make money to support my children.

In our first year of business, my company grossed 1.2 million dollars. I picked the cream of the crop from the previous employer, and they did a super job. I gave them bonuses and higher commission and it all was beautiful. Everyone was happy. We were flying high. I bought my own house, a new Cadillac and made $16,000 a month income. After three years I asked my partner to buy me out. That is a book, because it was not a good thing for me to have done. It was not easy to break the relationship with him. I was planning to get married to my third husband, and move to California, that was not a good enough reason for my partner to agree to a buyout.

Years went by and I was busy moving state to state with my husband and children. Not in business but going to college and getting my education. You see I had not been able to go to college in my early years. I got married at nineteen, had children immediately and the rest of life was difficult for a few years. My **memoir Breakaway: The Road To Freedom** is all about my life from five years old through marriage. No childhood, no teen life, no life at all.

I now had the opportunity to get my degree which I wanted badly all my life. My husband was able to support me; this was refreshing, and I loved it. When I had all those businesses I told you about, I was a high school dropout who received her diploma going to night school. That took ten years, but I did get my high school diploma finally. Now college, I was excited.

The company my husband worked for kept us on the move. He got promotion after promotion. I had to go from one university to another. In the process a lot of my credits were lost. Not all universities have the same classes or accept credits from others. Anyway, back to business.

Once we were settled again now in California, I opened a telephone store. I didn't know much about it, but one reason I wanted to do this was because I wanted a phone in my car. The car phones were the best, I wanted one installed in my car. They were too expensive to buy at the time, I could not afford it. So, the idea was born from the want and need to own a car phone. I called it Teletronix. I was great and still am great with naming products and companies. I love doing that. Teletronix was a store with home phones, pagers and car phones—we didn't have cell phones then. I contracted with a young man to install the car phones whenever I sold them. The home phones were all those decorator phones, leopards, cats, dogs, cars, candy bars, etc. I had so much fun with those. They were all so unique at the time. I sold and installed Siemens business phones too. The business grew and was doing very well. What happened next was devastating to me and that's when I closed shop.

I hired my son to work the shop so I could do other things. One day he called me and told me we were robbed. Two men came in with guns and stole pagers and some phones. He called the police while I was driving back to the store. I was concerned about my son. I did not care about the money or what they had stolen. I saw the two young African American teenage boys at the corner. I drove up to them, got out of the car and screamed at them. "Do you know how hard I have worked to open the store that you just robbed? You have no right to come in and threaten my son." I made a citizen's arrest with a gun pointing at them, to scare them, all I could think about was that they could have hurt my son. The police were on their way and saw me yelling at the teens. They stopped and I told them these were the robbers. They arrested the boys. I was thankful my son was alive and okay. We were both shaken by the whole incident.

The next day I called the landlord, told him what had happened and that I could not risk my son's life anymore. I asked him to let me out of the lease. Mr. Klein was a kind human being and released me. I sold off all the inventory and closed the doors. No amount of money was worth my son's life or my life.

The next business I thought of was selling precious stones like diamonds, emeralds and semi-precious stones like topaz, garnet, and peridot. I had special pieces made and I designed pieces to sell to doctors, lawyers and just about anyone in any price range. I had something for all customers. I never turned down an order. I had something for all budgets.

I went to the Gemological Institute in Santa Monica, California and received a certification in Color Stones, and Diamond grading. I took some other classes like semi-precious identifications, etc. It was fascinating. Every time I went to my doctor or my husband's doctor, I sold them jewelry. They loved the idea because their schedule did not permit them to shop at stores. It worked out great for them in their offices—special orders custom made at a great price.

They were thrilled and I was motivated. The fine jewelry business was fabulous. I called it Simone Designs and I worked it from home. I rented a mailbox at the UPS store, used that as my business address and had deliveries made there instead of my home. All deliveries and mail went to my UPS store address. I never used my home address for business.

The diamond business was very successful, too. I sold diamonds and emeralds more than any other stones. Big ticket items. I made great money with it; I had no overhead and I bought the merchandise when my customer gave me the deposit. I tried to collect half of the price to buy the stones. I never designed or ordered any piece without a nonrefundable deposit and one that would help pay for the most expensive stone. My money was never on the line or at stake.

We moved again after that. Another state, another business. After settling a while, I opened an accessory boutique. I sold hats, handbags, knockoff handbags, jewelry, etc. I leased a small space again, bought used glass cases for the jewelry and installed slat walls to hang all the handbags. Whenever I spotted a unique skirt or blouse, I included them in my inventory. The store attracted young girls and women who loved all the bling-bling stuff I had. I advertised, offered coupons and discounts. The store did very well. It was more of a hobby for me since my husband was a good provider and I didn't have to worry about money as much. I still wanted to make my own money of course. After a few businesses I realized I was more interested in the challenge and the conquest of the businesses I started. It was a challenge to open them and once I did, the conquest was made. I enjoyed selling them and moving on. Everyday my brain has new ideas for business. I can't do everything. Now, I am an author, podcaster, YouTube Host, and actress. I will have to choose one real soon.

Chapter 2

What Is Your Dream?

We all have dreams that get lost in life. We lose them for many reasons. Let me tell you this: Without the dreams there is no passion. That is my opinion. We must have a dream, and from the dream passion is born. I have learned that the hard way. My dream has always been to be an actress. It took years to get the dream realized. I am now an actress, an author and talk show host. But for years my dream was to make a lot of money, to be an entrepreneur and give people things they had never seen or things they needed at a fair price. I was never greedy except for one time in my life. That was a lesson well learned and another book at a later date. Maybe.

What is your dream? Have you forgotten it? Has it disappeared? Have hard times made you file it away in some corner of your mind? Do you think it's impossible to have that dream? Have you thought that you can't do it no matter how you try? Don't be afraid to do it, don't let others say you can't do it, take the risk. If you fail, try again and again until you succeed. Never give up.

Time to open the files, dust them off. Write down what your dream is. Now, write down what you want to do about it and what it will take to do it. Think small, no need to think big right now. Start with the small details. You need to see if the passion for that dream comes forth. Do you feel excited looking and the list of possibilities? Is there a rush, nervousness, can you, do it? YES, you can do it. I did it. All my businesses except for the vitamin company were started with less than one thousand dollars. So, don't say "I can't." WOW! Think of your own business. Be your own boss. You can do it. Dropout or college graduate. The possibilities are endless. I can't tell you how many businesses I think of everyday and know that I can do it. But I am only one person. I can't do everything, although I'm still trying!

Passion is the key to success. This is what will drive you to where you want to go and where you want to be in your life. I read somewhere these three things are what we need for success: passion, patience, and persistence. We all want to be winners. Nobody likes to lose. Life is what it is. We have winners and losers, love and hate, right and wrong, etc.

There is opposition for everything and anything. Nothing or no one in life is perfect, keep that in mind and you won't be disappointed. As my children always remind me: Mom if you don't expect things from people, you won't be hurt. That is so true. No expectations. Just live your dream, have the passion to get started, the patience to get it done and to do it right, and the persistence to stick to it no matter what. It takes time to accomplish things. Good things take time. If it happens quickly, it does not last. The longer it takes to succeed, the better it will be and the longer it will last. It's like red wine, the longer it ages the better it gets. I know you have heard this before. I love this quote. Wish I had thought it and created it.

You have your list of dreams, your list of what it will take to get started. Go down the list and figure out what it will take to open the doors, website, or blog. Nowadays we have more than a storefront for possibilities. We have internet. That opens eBay, Craigslist, websites, blogs, distribution companies, etc. Figure out the best way to market your dream.

Do you want or need people to walk into a store space, office space, garage, or whatever? Does your product need to be displayed, touched, smelled, or listened to? Do you want a website? You will need this anyway, so that is your store too. How much money do you need? Can you start your dream with a website or maybe a store on eBay? With these options you wouldn't need much inventory. Maybe a piece or two at a time. When one sells replace it with another immediately. Once you have that figured out, you can make the dream come true by starting out small and gradually increasing inventory.

The good news is you have the dream started and the passion rolling out. See, it's not so hard to do. But wait, there is more to think of before starting any of these projects. There is the legal stuff. You must be legal to prevent any problems with IRS. So, let's talk about that next. This is very important.

Chapter 3

How to be Legal at a Low Cost

Many think that they must incorporate first and spend thousands to get started with getting their legal business name and other necessary documents. Not true. All you need initially is a fictitious name like Teletronix, Foxee' Lady, Simone Designs, etc. Figure out what you would like to call your business. It's always good to name it with some connection of what you are doing in the title. Kind of a product recognition of what you are selling. For example, KS Accessories—we know it's accessories of some kind. KS Cafe, well, we know it's food. KS Marketing may describe a service like a distribution center or maybe a service.

You have the name decided and the shorter the better. One or two words are best and easier to remember. Before filing, if you do not get a physical building or store location, go to the UPS store or any other similar facility. Open a box in your business name. Be sure the address is a street address not a post office box number. The reason being that you cannot get deliveries at a post office box. The street address is better too because it looks to wholesalers like you have a physical store. Some wholesalers are reluctant to selling wholesale to anyone who does not have a storefront.

Having a street address alleviates that and them asking the question. The best part is that the deliveries are accepted Monday through Saturday no matter where you are. Someone is always there protecting your packages until you pick them up. The next step is looking up and calling your local county clerk's office to find out when it's open, usually Monday through Friday till 5 pm. Find out the cost to file a fictitious name and the address to get there, use your GPS if you have one. File your fictitious name and you are in business.

Oh, but one more thing, you need a resale number for purchasing wholesale goods to sell retail. This must be from the state office called the Comptroller's Office. Every state is different. Find out from the County Clerk where this is. They are very helpful in answering questions. Don't be afraid to ask any question by calling any state office or city hall. They know the steps and who you need to call and where to go. You have filed your fictitious name and now you have your resale number that is in your business name. You will need to present the fictitious name certificate to get the resale number as well as any other accounts which we will discuss as we go along.

The next place you need to go to is the bank. Go to your favorite local bank and talk to the new accounts person and have your fictitious name certificate available. This is proof you are legal, and you are who you say you are. Open the bank account with free checking. Most banks today have free business checking tied to a savings account or a credit card or a limited balance in your account. It is great. You have opened your checking account, and you are now in business and you are legal. Get familiar with the bank and all the employees, know them by name. It is important to do this. One day you may need a loan or help of some sort. When you know them by name and say hello to them occasionally, it makes a big difference in how you are treated. I have a relationship with everyone in my bank. I can call and ask for almost anything and I know they will take good care of me.

They want my business, and they want my money; they need me more than I need them. I am the customer. Without you and me the bank would be closed. Remember that.

So once you have all the above completed, then decide whether you should have a website or a physical location along with a website to start your dream business. It depends on what you want to do and how soon you want it to be done.

A website is going to be necessary no matter which you choose. You need to get a web designer or learn how to do it yourself. There are websites that offer easy web building, and the server fee is low like $5 a month to publish it on Google. At the end of the book, I will list several web companies you can look up as well as other ideas.

You have selected a storefront and a space, hopefully it was not too big. Don't start too big unless you have too much money and need to spend it! Before leasing, plan your space design. How much space do you need? How much product do you need to fill the space? Some retail lease spaces require you to do the build out. Build out is where you only get the studs, the air space. You have to hire someone to drywall it, etc. You can do it yourself if you are a handyman. Most places will give you so much money per square foot to help with the expense. Be sure to find out how much they will pay and how much it will cost you. I have always leased a place finished. I do not like buildouts, but that's just me. I'd rather spend my time decorating.

Don't forget you can negotiate most of the time to have the lessor, the owner, do the buildout, or give you up to three months' rent free. Negotiate. It doesn't hurt to ask, they can only say no, or they might give you what you want. You'll never know unless you ask.

It is time to look at a lease. Be sure to read it carefully and if you are not sure what to do or do not understand it clearly, find a business lawyer for a small fee to read it and explain it to you; it's worth it believe me. If you sign and not know what you signed or missed something, it can cost you at the end. Always read the fine print. Take your time reading the lease. This is a legal document.

Get a lawyer to read it if you can. It's not worth the risk, unless it is simply written without much legal jargon and there are no questions. I mean simple third grade level. Negotiate the lease to fit your terms, most of the time the lessor needs to lease and is willing to lease for one year instead of three. If you get one year, have a clause where you will have the option to lease two or more years without an increase in rent or a minimal amount may be negotiated up to a certain percentage depending on the cost-of-living rate, perhaps not more than two percent the second year. Negotiate.

You signed the lease and that is the last step to being legal. Now you have a lot more to do. Hopefully, you have placed an order for your goods to be delivered on a certain date or you know what to order and from whom to order. Plan AHEAD. When you know more about the date of opening you will be ready. The next step is equipment to show off the inventory.

Chapter 4

Equipping Your Store

*H*ere we are. We have the dream, the idea, the name, the accounts, the product, the website, the store, the lease, and now we need the equipment to show off our inventory. Depending on what you are going to stock, figure out what pieces you need.

Get the equipment you need to stock your products. There are retail equipment stores all over the USA. Look online and most have free shipping. Find the deals for what you need. Don't overdo it. Don't overbuy. Only buy the equipment you need. Less is better for now, again unless you have lots of money, then buy whatever you want and stock it up. Now, if you install slat walls with special hangers, it not only looks great, but it's organized and keeps your inventory off the floor. Use floor displays only for bigger items. Every item on the market pretty much has a display made for it. Shop around and get the best price you can.

If you are building an online store, of course you eliminate the above displays, but you still may need them in the storeroom, garage, basement or whatever just to keep things off the floor and handy. In any of these locations you can get away with less. You may want to buy used equipment or hand-made equipment to display, shelve or store your inventory if appearance doesn't matter that much.

Equipment is no problem really, although some of it is costly. It depends where you have the business. Target and Walmart have cheap bookcases that work fabulously for books, inventory of knickknacks, dolls, plates, small crystal gift items and many others. You would be surprised. I have used these bookcases for handbags and gift items in my store. I had black ones and white ones. Your color decor publicly is important too. Color has a lot to do with inviting the customers in. Is it appealing? Will they feel good coming into your store?

While I'm about inventory, you may want to consider having your inventory items drop shipped, especially for large orders. The distributor ships directly to the customer and you get a nice paycheck weekly monthly or quarterly. You avoid handling and shipping. Again, it depends on the contracts you sign with your suppliers; get a lawyer to read the fine print. Have him or her modify agreements if there's something between the lines that needs clarification.

Now you have your business ready to go. Sales come in and stock is monitored. Don't wait until you are completely out of stock with an item before you purchase. At least have two of everything, if one sells replenish. You do not want to lose sales because you are out of stock. Customers will buy somewhere else.

You need to target your customers. My store was aimed mainly at women, although men did shop there, but the merchandise was all feminine stuff. I painted walls a smoky lavender and trimmed in white. The furnishings and counters were white and any metal on displays was brushed silver not chrome. I thought it was inviting, fresh, serene, and made you feel good to be in my store. The better they feel the more they will spend. But again, don't do too much; be minimalist rather than gaudy in your approach. You always can adjust things.

The very first thing you should do is buy a computer, a printer, a copier with scanner and fax included. Also, a land line or a cell phone. These are necessary for anything you do. Be careful buying used here; better to buy new and get the warranties. If you don't have the money for a computer, perhaps you can rent or borrow one for a while. But get these tools as soon as you can. You cannot operate in today's world without them. Communication is the key to any business success.

Chapter 5

How to Find Manufacturers

Manufacturers are a lot easier to locate now than ever before. The internet is filled with them from all over the world—manufacturers of every kind, every sort, every size. Be careful when dealing with anyone in the United States as well as abroad. Check their references, find out who is dealing with them and if they are happy, ask if their customer service is good. Don't be afraid to ask questions. If you don't ask, you may wish you had later.

I have found that manufacturers do overcharge on shipping in some cases. Try to negotiate and open a shipping account with FedEx, DHL, UPS, and others. Check rates and see who is best. Who has the most reasonable rates for air, land, or sea, international and domestic? You will want to have the most efficient shipping partner.

Virtually all industries have conventions where manufacturers, distributors, designers, sales agents, etc. are represented. Often you can make all the connections you need under one roof for just about anything man can make. You can resource suppliers online as well. Just google intuitively for conventions or the specific product line you are wanting to sell. Wholesalers want your business. Remember, they need you as much as you need them so find the best deal. It's a competitive world out there.

Chapter 6

Your Greatest Resource

Are you doing something you know? Have you educated yourself about the business, the product? The more knowledge about the product, the more success you will have. There are books, videos, YouTube, online websites, and podcasts to help you learn more about what you already know. You have to get out of the box and learn something new. That's another way of saying that you need to expand your knowledge. Stay fresh and current in your line of business. Know what the competition is doing. Don't worry about them, but If you hear of something new, do your research, find out who's doing what and how successful they are.

You might consider buying a franchise. Many are expensive but you might find a good deal in your area of interest. Entry-level franchises sometimes don't require much to get started. These can be found online as well.

There are many businesses that you can work at from home: jewelry, cosmetics, crafts, novelties, lingerie, toys, housewares, almost anything you want. Check these out. I know someone who sold used cars from home and made a decent living doing it. Some businesses require a minimum investment or purchase of minimum inventories. Pay the fee, but the rest is up to you. Depending on your business, you can almost always count on friends or relatives to get you going. Build your contact list. Make new friends. Contact everyone you know who might be interested in your products. Don't prejudge either. If someone you know doesn't want to buy right away, they may know someone who will.

Get Facebook, X , LinkedIn and Amazon Store, TikTok, and Instagram accounts. These are very important in getting your business name and products out to the whole USA and the world. Check the other companies like yours and see how they advertise. Duplicate as much as you can without being too obvious. More about platforms later in this book.

Another idea: If you do not know anything about a particular business but love an idea or love the product, contact someone who does have the knowledge. Start a partnership or hire them as an independent contractor. Hire them on an as needed basis to help you get started. There is always a way.

You might consider an internet business. My friend Debbie has one where she created a very successful business helping authors launch their books. They pay her $300-$5,000 to do this. It depends on the package that they want. The higher the cost, the bigger the launch. She gets them to be number one on amazon.com in no time flat. I mean in one day; she manages to help them sell books that day more than anyone else on Amazon.

The author then is #1 top-selling author for that day and can use that on their advertising. In some cases, it can stay at #1 for weeks. Another internet business is one where you help people like myself network. You get paid to find friends, add friends, write status on FB, Myspace, Twitter, LinkedIn, etc.

For this type of business, you can charge from $25-$100 a month depending how many days and hours clients want to be networked. You put your services in nice packages, bundle them and offer them online on your networks to get business. Think about this, it is a great way to make money to buy bread and butter at first and maybe later the car you always wanted. Hmmmm, good idea. Start small, be honest, care about the person you are helping with networking and word of mouth will make you a successful person.

The good thing about being in business for yourself is that you can set your own hours and never have to punch a clock. But whatever you do, make sure you schedule your time and keep you your schedule. It's very easy to work either too little or too much. The resources are out there but remember this: You are your greatest resource. Take care of yourself!

Chapter 7

Do You Need Investors?

*I*nvestors always want a piece of the pie. You may want to share your success with investors to get the money you need for startup or expansion, but always be sure you have more shares, a larger percentage than anyone else, otherwise you lose control of the business you started. Here you definitely need a lawyer. Now on TV you can watch *Shark Tank* to learn how to ask for investors and get well known. You might even try to get on the show yourself. That would be great advertising for you. I love that show and watch it every week.

Figure out how much you need to borrow, how much you want to give in return. Sometimes you can have what are called silent partners. They give the money, get a percentage of the business as a royalty for a length of time and that's it. They do not become a part of the company or tell you how to run the business. They are in it just for the investment, even if they lose every penny; it's a risk they take. They want passive income. You would not be liable to return any monies to the investors in this case unless you signed a contract stating that you would. Most do not. Organize a limited liability company with the Secretary of State and get investors under your LLC. Again, you can do this yourself if you're pretty savvy about business, but most people will want to consult an attorney. Don't consult just any attorney though. Make sure they are credentialed in business and are board certified. There is much to learn about LLC and incorporating. Investors feel more comfortable if you have an attorney supporting you.

You will also need a CPA if you seek out investors. Tax laws change all the time, and they are very complicated. Unless you are an expert yourself, you must get help in this area. The last thing you want to have is a problem with the IRS. This is especially true if you depend on investors to help you finance your business. If you are seeking investors, it's very likely that you have already been in business for a while or you will have to have a very hot idea. The kind of investor you want is someone who not only has plenty of money but someone who might be of value to you in other ways, preferably someone who is very familiar and has a lot of experience in the business you're in.

Whatever business you're in, if possible don't make it complicated. Make it simple. You can make a new cookie recipe and sell it if you know how to market, and you have knowledge about why your cookie is better than others. If you are qualified, you may want to start a more complicated business, but that might mean that you must go to school (not a bad idea!), get certified or get a license. You can be successful in this way as well as long as you remember this formula:

Passion + Patience + Persistence = Success

Finally, focus on others not yourself. Think of the customer first. Never give up. Learn how to deal with failure. Get up and do it again if you lose the first time. As someone has said: Success is a journey not a destination. Enjoy the process. Congratulations on your new business! I wish you all success and prosperity! Be happy, be positive and don't let anyone tell you that you can't do it. YOU CAN DO IT!

Chapter 8

Ideas For Startups

1. **Pet Sitting**. It is a great business if you are a stay-at-home mom or just someone who wants extra income. This can be done at any age from 18 and up to 100. It requires the licenses for business and other things like being bonded and insured. Start in your neighborhood. Let neighbors know you have started a pet sitting business by placing a business card or flyer on their door. Dogs generally require a walk outdoors and of course need to go outdoors to do their business. Dog sitting may take you forty-five minutes to an hour to walk, feed and give love to. Cat sitting takes about twenty to half an hour to feed, clean litter and give love to. You can do both or specialize in dogs or cats, depends on which you like best. Charges are anywhere from $15 to $30 an hour. Check other pet sitter sites and see what they do and what they charge. You can be competitive but be reasonable. It is a great business if you love animals. I don't advise doing this unless you love animals. If you love dogs, be a dog sitter only. If you love cats, be a cat only sitter. If you love both, do both. Set a radius of distance that you will travel to do this. You may consider after awhile that this is a great business and hire others to help you to expand the territory.

2. **Jewelry**. Make a unique style of jewelry. Start a store on eBay, a Facebook page displaying your jewelry. Website store to sell your jewelry or any other craft you make. Sell beads wholesale at a profit to other jewelry makers. See FB and eBay for ideas on style and stores.

3. **eBay**. I have a friend who has opened a store on eBay and is quite successful doing this. She has had it now for ten

years. Open an eBay store where you can buy clearance items that some stores mark down to one dollar up to five dollars. Regular prices may have been as high as $150. This might appeal to the international market and USA market for someone who cannot afford full price. Leave tags on garments or merchandise until they are sold. But be sure to remove when sold. Buy what you like in case it does not sell. With tags on you may return to store for a refund. Check their policies for returned clearance items. If you bought it for a $1.00 on clearance, start at a reasonable price where it looks like a great deal. Judge by the markdowns the store made. It all depends on the item. You may be able to get more. Some items look very expensive, so go from there. Start high and then mark it down, put it on sale at a profit. Try to at least make a profit of three times the cost.

4. **Used Books**. Specialize in what may be of interest. Website or eBay. For example: Books on boating, tools, how to books, filmmaking books, acting books, etc. Go to book clearances, used bookstores, Half Price Books, find bargains, start small, add as you need to. With books and garments, you can buy as needed. Start with a small inventory, see what happens.

There are bargains everywhere now. Whatever you like most of the time the public will like. Specialize or mix with other ideas. You decide what is best for you. What can you do better than someone else. Can you sing, play an instrument, teach others in your home or theirs. Can you cook? Teach others how to cook, build websites, online marketing. A lot of young people today do not know how to cook. Create an online magazine or newsletter. Get businesses to advertise for a fee. Start small and gradually increase it. Create a line of nutritional supplements or one popular supplement and sell it. So many things to do and some make money quickly and some slowly. It takes time. All things worth having take time and they last longer. Be patient and be happy. Love what you do and what you are doing. It is contagious and it will sell.

Chapter 9

Who's The Boss?

I am the BOSS of my life next to God being my spiritual BOSS. I have done so much on my own, I really don't need a man to take care of me financially. It would be nice if I had a man who was understanding and not threatened.

I am constantly thinking of ways to make money, not to be filthy rich, but to be able to and buy whatever my heart desires.

Another adventure in having my own business, is whenever I needed something where the cost is too high, I find out how I can have that business to get what I want or need at wholesale. That is the theme throughout my life, if retail is too high, get into the business you need at that moment. So, when I moved into my mansion which I don't have now, we needed blinds throughout the house. It was a new house and we were the first time buyers. My husband then made a lot of money, but we didn't feel like spending $50,000 on blinds. The house was two stories, the windows were floor to ceiling and when you looked out, it seemed as if you were outside. That's how big they were. We needed remote controls for this house. I researched different vendors, and found Hunter Douglas had exactly what we needed and wanted. I went to the county clerk's office for the fictious name and I called it, Fancy Blinds. I had my husband measure all of the windows, and I placed my order. Instead of paying $50,000 we ended up paying $20,000. We had windows all over the house, as well as Atrium doors which also needed blinds.

After that, I stayed in it for awhile, helped friends get blinds they needed with a major discount. I got tired of the window shade business and moved on. Just quit.

After that ordeal, we needed so many things for our new home. We needed plants, big plants. Our ceiings were high, like 22' and so we needed tall trees, palm trees, Fica trees, flowers in big huge pots, made of synthetic material that looked real. We

39

didn't want plastic, we wanted silk. I got into the decorating business and became an interior designer. We needed furniture in some of the rooms, and book cases, and wall hangings, paintings, and art work…

I became a designer. I found what I needed by going to the most expensive furniture stores in Texas. I looked at labels for the manufacturer who made the silk plants and trees. I researched and found them, called them, asked for their catalog after introducing myself as a designer. They wanted my license number, and my sales tax ID. I had it all ready. I was so excited! I ordered at wholesale all the plants and trees I needed and wanted. After that, family and friends loved my purchases, they bought from me and of course I made a profit that really ended up paying for my plants. I did give them a huge discount though.

There's a huge mark-up in retail, especially in the high-end furniture stores I went to. This was so much fun for me. I loved the challenge of the research, the findings, and the buying. After that I was ready for a new challenge, what should that be?

Chapter 10

Marketing

My husband needed to market his organic chocolate and gum business. He had no clue how to start. Well, Nadia to the rescue. I started a business called, "Dynamic Marketing." I had cards printed, and websites, and all the things needed to market his business.

I began my research on learning the ins and the outs. I learned how to market and where. I had him place ads in the newspapers, magazines, and online. I hired a crew of people to call grocery store managers and find out who in the business is in charge of ordering. I had my crew call health food stores and drug stores.

It was fun again! The marketing started to show signs of success. My husband was thrilled. But as you know by my personality already, I was bored. I met the challenge, and I was ready for another conquest. Yet, I had to see this through, it was too soon for me to give up the ship.

My husband had to rent a warehouse and hire a staff to ship product as soon as the orders came in. We hired a receptionist, a CPA to handle all the invoices and taxes, we hired a payroll company to issue pay checks to all the people we employed. Things were going well, and we were both very happy with the results. I began created ADS myself, for newspaper ads, magazine ads, and I was pretty happy with my artistic creations. We sold a few thousand dollars worth of items within a six month period. The best sales goal was achieved. I don't know what happened, but things got slow a bit, my husband was frustrated again. I just let it go. I was not going to continue marketing and be the fall guy. I wanted my husband to help me and do some of the work too. He gave up, I gave up, and after two years the business was dissolved.

You cannot always achieve and be successful, but you don't give up. You keep trying until you make it. Honestly, I didn't have his business in my heart, it was not me, not my cupcake. It has to be your dream, your passion to succeed.

Chapter 11

Forgotten Adventure

My next adventure Whew!!! I've got to tell you this story, because I forgot to tell you earlier. At the age of twenty-five, married to a man with child support, kept me from having my needs met as well as my children's. No house, no real good food, no boy scout uniforms, no uniforms for any activity my sons wanted to participate in. So, I thought of a good idea. My neighbors and friends at the apartment building where we resided were the Detroit Lions players and their families. I met them, I was in the same building of two of them and the rest in another building. I met the wives, we became friends and I talked to them about my idea. They were so excited and they said they would be my very first students. Are you ready for my idea?

It was to start teaching my cultural beautiful, artistic, and graceful Belly Dancing!

I placed an ad in the local newspaper for private lessons at $15 half an hour. I had three of the Football wives already in. I received a call from the high school asking me if I would be interested in teaching belly dance in the evenings to adult women. I agreed to a meeting and the arrangement was as follows: Teach at 7pm for an hour, each woman will pay $18 for six weeks. I woud receive $10 for each student the school the $8. I agreed. Over one-hundred women signed up. The school had to add more nights or two classes the same evening. 25 women to a class. They set up with my agreement two classes on Tuesday, and two on Thursday, at 7pm and at 8pm.

It was amazing, there were more calls for more classes in other school districts. I was in demand. The word was out and the three school systems were thrilled. I was driving every night and teaching with the exception of the weekends.

I had to think of way to get it all, and not drive an hour each way, I was very tired by the end of each class and the drive home was too long. Five days a week, some schools were an hour away, some half an hour away, it was always a long night for me five nights a week. I had to find a way to have all these women come to me.

The light bulb in my brain came on. I needed to lease a building and have my own Belly Dance Studio. I could teach smaller classes, I would give my students the same arrangement and pricing, I would get the whole pie, the whole $18 and they would drive to me. I could even open a boutique in the studio and sell all things belly dance.

I discussed it with my best friend Jenny, she thought it was brilliant. "How do you do it, Nadia? I am so impressed you are the smartest girlfriend and I love you!" I loved my friend Jenny. We were together a lot, shopping, traveling and getting in trouble with our husbands. Jenny's children always say to this day, "our mom was shy, quiet and sweet, and never got into trouble, till she met you". Jenny and I always got a kick from that and laughed at it. Jenny and I had lots of fun. First of all, I had to ask all three hundered or so students if I gave them the same price would they make the trip once a week to my studio, they all said "YES!" So, Jenny helped me find a building and we did in Auburn Heights, MI.

It was a stand alone, charming old building with a huge storefront window, it was perfect.

I went to the final nights of the last week at the schools, and enrolled my students at my studio. I gave them two weeks off to do what they needed and so I could prepare my studio to an inviting place for my students to love coming too. I was excited!
I negotiated the lease terms and leased it for three years Jenny helped me in the two weeks to get ready. I had a carpenter wall up a room for me about 300sq.ft. so I could create and decorate an inviting boutique. I got that up and starting stocking it up with costumes, danskin tights and bodysuits for practice, belly dance albums, finger cymbals, drums, jewelry, ankle jewelry, head jewelry anything and everything that was something a belly dancer would want. Jenny and I completed it all, and we were ready for fun.

Chapter 12

The Studio

*T*he studio opened and one thing led to another. I began my teaching courses, beginners, intermediate, and advanced. The girls had fun, and they kept coming and new students came from my newspaper ads, word of mouth, and all the times I was on TV and in the newspapers, I never had an empty time or space. I was elated. At the advance level I held and produced recitals for the friends and relatives of my students to come and see the progress of their loved one. I created tickets and charged $5 to each person to come to the recital. I had a full house. My students loved it! The beginners and intermediate were all excited for the day they would perform for their friends and family.

I am showing you the progression of success and how one thing led to another. The more plans I had the more money I made.

I hired a professional seamstress to make professional belly dance costumes for any student who wanted to have one and wear it at the recital. Of course, I made a profit off each one. Every costume cost my student at least $300 I made a $100 off each order. My seamstress was amazing and happy to have a steady income of $200 or more. As the costume price increased so did my profit. My boutique was busy too. I bought albums for $3 and sold them for $10-$15 dollars each. I made money every way I could. I made so much money my husband began to feel inferior. So, beware of that. I emasculated my husband, not on purpose, he just could not provide for my needs or the needs of my children. He was a punch the clock guy, he depended on someone else to give him raises and to help him earn more money. I was not the punch the clock girl. I loved making my own money, my way, and doing things I love to do. I love and still today, I would take a commissioned pay any day instead of a paycheck or salary.

Commission makes you work harder and when you do you make more money and you get paid for it right there and then.

Salaries are limited, no matter how good you are, you may not get a raise for a year or five years down the road after you've helped your company become successful. Once they give you a raise then they fire you if you don't perform the way you did when they paid you less. You can't win. As you get older, they replace you with someone younger at half the pay. I have heard this happen so much in the years 2000 and beyond.

It's a sad situation. Be your own boss and you'll make more money than any salary. However, you must know what you want and how to do it. If you fail keep trying, I encourage you not to give it up. There are so many tools today to get help. Internet, seminars, webinars, courses on Udemy, I love Udemy. I have purchased at least forty courses at least $10 each. They are lifetime access. I love learning. I will talk further about this.

Chapter 13

Online Courses

I have no reason to tell you this, except it's a great teaching tool. I am talking about **Udemy.** I love Udemy! It's an App get it downloaded now. It's something you want to keep. Don't' spend more than $15 on any course, make a list on Udemy of what you want. On Udemy app it's called a "Wishlist."
If the courses you need are over $15 make a Wishlist, add them in and went the price of that course is $10 or $15 you can buy it. Udemy reduces the rates to most of them and they are always available for a rate reduction. If you're in a hurry, at least wait 2-3 weeks and they will go on sale. It's up to you when you buy.

You can learn about any business from A-Z if Udemy doesn't have it, no one does. I bought things and courses to learn from learning Audio recording to French speaking course all the way to learn how to build a website on WordPress.

Ok, don't laugh, I have courses like, drawing, painting, calligraphy, speaking, French, guitar, ukulele, how to sell film, how to cast a bankable actor, filmmaking, copywriting, Novel writing, Fiction writing, blogging, songwriting, screenwriting, see how many things I am going to do in my life! there's more, but I am not going to list them all. Remember I have forty courses. LOL one at a time. I may not do all of them, but I am learning about them. I love learning.

Another Course I just stumbled on, and the young man seems sincere. **Brendon Burchard**. He's the Godfather of online training. He looks so young. But that is his claim and I believe him. He is highly respected, and his company is called "Influencer Pro." I bought his courses to learn how to market my books and other things. I am an influencer on Amazon, and I need to know what to do. This is the latest venture. I bought into go.influencerpro.com, check it out. I get nothing for this information, I should though. LOL.

I am listening now at his videos and learning a lot from him. I'd say just what I've learned from one video I got my money's worth. I must practice what he is telling me, and how he's telling me to do it. To get more sales, more followers, etc.

I am doing this, writing this book, and getting ready to publish one other book I've written. I don't let any time stop me from living or doing what I need or want to do.

My do window forward is shorter than the I done it window behind me.

I think the life of suppression in my early years and in marriage, I feel I missed out on living. Now in this stage of my life, I want to do as much as I can to catch up on all things I missed. Can you relate?

Chapter 14

Assistance for Anything Business

*T*here are so many wonderful courses and webinars that don't cost an arm and a leg. I for one do not like to pay hundreds or thousands of dollars for courses. That is why I choose **Udemy.** I wait for sales of $10-$20 for my interests, and they do happen, just add on the App **Wishlist,** and wait. Another wonderful helpful sight is **Fiverr.**

OMG! These sellers on Fiverr are geniuses. They are from different countries, and they speak and write many languages. From Africa to Zimbabwe. Many are from Pakistan, Bangladesh, USA, although the USA ones are more expensive. The ones from the third world are very reasonable and they do an excellent job. Fiverr is a rating system for both the seller and the buyer. If you're happy you write a review, if the seller was happy working with you, he/she writes a review abut you. It's really an excellent site. I wish I had thought of it.

Upwork, is another one that is like Fiverr, but they offer different kinds of sellers, and buyers. I think it would behoove you to download or go to the websites and browse each one, see which has the fit for your needs.

I mentioned online courses too. I love those especially if they are lifetime access. There were a couple that were not, so I don't buy those anymore. I feel if I pay for a course, I should always have access throughout my life. You always want that, because you want to refresh your memory about certain things and maybe go do more research or check something out that may have been presented toy you and you need to know how to navigate it. You want it to be like an Encyclopedia Set on your computer to access day or night. There are so many conflicts and obstacles in life, it's hard to take time to read, write or review. You must take and allow precious time for yourself to learn, to comprehend and put it to practice seeing how it really works and how it will benefit you.

There are so many days and months where I think I am going to be able to do things, and somehow something always happens to distract me.
That's why we need Lifetime Access for anything we buy to learn at our pace at the times that are convenient for us, not the author of the videos. Just be sure that it's really for you and that you will enjoy watching or listening to the videos or audio tapes. Be sure it's what you need and want, that it's your passion, your determination, your heartfelt, I AM DOING THIS!

In between all this learning, take a break after an hour or so, play a game on the computer, read something fun, or listen to music. Get away from it for at least thirty minutes. It will help refresh you. It's hard to stay at the computer for longer than hour and it's unhealthy. You must get up and stand, take a walk outside, take deep breaths, pray, enjoy nature, be happy, be grateful and it all comes together at the right time for you. I do this every day, I work one hour writing, then I go outside listen to the birds sing, smell the fresh air, and I talk to God. I thank him for my family, my friends, my health, my life, and everything he has blessed me with. If not for God, I would not be alive or here on this earth doing what I love. Be grateful, be encouraged, be inspired. Be love to all whom you know, and they will always remember that love no matter what happens in your lifetime. Go on do what you want to do, it's your dream. Start now!

Chapter 15

Networking!

etwork!! When you start researching your dream business and after you've began the business journey, whatever it is, you must Network! Find out about meetups in your area, go to Meetups.com or get the App. It's Free! Join book clubs, social clubs, film clubs, Church clubs, go to church, meet people, that is the best place ever, to meet people that have something in common with you from the start, they are spiritual. Go to parties, meet friends of the family, start a conversation by complimenting the other person whom you just met, ask their name, find out who they are, what they do, and that is the beginning of a possible support system and friend to help you promote your business or to be a customer. Who knows, yet you have a new friend. Friends are valuable resources. If they believe in your journey, they will be there for you.

I love people! I love meeting people. Success depends on people, how you meet them, how you connect with them, and sincere you are with them. Being there for them when they need you is always a gratitude give back. If it were not for my friends, I would feel alone, as if I were stranded on a desert island with no one around, just me. That's an awful feeling. When Covid hit all of us in the United States, I felt alone in my isolation from seeing or being with my friends and family. Oh, we called, and we zoomed, but that does not do it for me. I need the physical touch, the presence. I missed that so much, two years of alone time for the first time in my life was good in the sense I found out who I really was, what I really wanted and what I needed to do. What a revelation! Being alone for two years! I found out stuff about me. I learned so much about my personality and why I said and did the things that I did in my life. I must tell you about that, because we all have patterns in our lives that we carry from childhood. Who knew? I have a source that will blow your mind, will help you learn so much about yourself that it feels like you just woke up from a deep sleep you didn't even know you were sleeping, you were Sleepwalking, YES! That's it Sleepwalking!

Back to Networking, I get off track sometimes. When you go to a store, network with the cashiers, the salesclerk, the manager, all the people that work in the store are great resources. Go into a bookstore, meet the manager, know who they are, introduce yourself. He/she is a great asset, they will order your book and add it to the inventory, sign you up for a book signing in the store. I've done many book signings, I love it! I met my customers and signed my book for them, and the best thing is they shared their story with me and how they related to my story. See, they related. They shared my book with their friends and family. Why? Because they related to my story. They networked my book with all the persons in their life. The best customer ever!

Be sure to sign up on Facebook, Twitter now X, Instagram, YouTube, Tumblr, Email, Blog, Threads, and more. Find out which one is best for you and the business you will start. Make friendships online, keep it clean if it's business, keep it business. Don't' add personal family stuff on business networks. Keep family and personal just that, Personal. I think this is fun to do and gain more friends, meet new friends this way from anywhere in the world. It's a beautiful time to learn about the cultures of the world and maybe you will stumble on an idea from another land and peoples. Who knows.

Chapter 16

Platforms; Best Live Streaming!

WOW! I am finding new platforms right now too! This is great! Researching for this book has led me to new platforms that I will use. The online platforms are exciting, they are what you need for different reasons. Platforms online make it easy for you get educated, or to train, they are a management system online. It can be easier and cheaper to manage any business venture you take. You will be able to reach people all around the globe with platforms. With computers, and smart phones, we can access platforms and learn no matter where we are and where we go. It's all right there in our sweet little palm. The statements and platform ABOUT are accurately taken from their individual websites, I thought that would be easier for all of us to understand each function of each platform. However, please access each one and do your own research and find your platform or platforms to help you in your venture.

So, let's begin.

The best live streaming platforms are as follows:

YouTube is amazing, I have a channel, please subscribe to it, I have all of them listed at end of this book. I want to see you on all of them and let me know you read this book. I want to connect with you.

Connect yourself on YouTube, build an audience by live streaming your business, your hobby, your interests, or have guests that you love and want to learn from. At some point your channel can quality for monetization. Read the rules on YouTube and see where you can benefit. YouTube now has Two Billion users every month! Be one of them, be the best. You can do it.

FACEBOOK LIVE!

Facebook has a **global base of 2.7 billion users monthly active users. Facebook has restrictions on monetization's and time limits for live streaming. You can broadcast from mobile or desktop.**

LINKEDIN LIVE

LinkedIn is now a full-fledged content creation platform. There are articles, videos, and live videos from influencers, brands, and other professionals, that might fit into your line or industry 93 percent of business-to-business use LinkedIn for their marketing needs. use LinkedIn for organic social marketing. LinkedIn users have <u>twice as much buying power</u> as the average internet user. LinkedIn has no monetization.

TWITCH

If you're a gamer, this is the streaming platform that might be what you need. In the Q3 of 2022 Twitch had 5.71 billion watcher hours globally. Twitch does have several monetization options that might be worth looking into. They also have a Chatting Channel that is very popular with gamers. Check it out!

TIK TOK LIVE

TIK TOK, is geared towards viral videos. The audience and users here are mainly Gen Z. It's a free App and Free platform. Your video can be as long as 60 minutes on Tik Tok. There has been controversy with this App and it's origin possibly from China. Check this carefully and see if it fits you and your video needs.

INSTAGRAM LIVE

Instagram began as a photo sharing platform, but now it's more than that. It's a live stream platform. Instagram has become the social media live streaming platform that allows you to sell products in-stream. IG has a <u>live shopping</u> feature, you can monetize with in-stream ads and donation badges from viewers. Keep in mind with Instagram Live is that most users can only stream from a mobile device via the Instagram app. It's not compatible with computers, or giving users the ability to post links to connect from IG to another website or streaming site. You must post with a photo or reel to connect on IG.

Well, I guess that's it for live streaming, However, there is Streamyard, and **Zoom**, which I didn't find in my research. I use Zoom for my live streaming. I love Zoom because it has virtual backgrounds, and you can choose the skin tone you want on your videos. Zoom saves your video and you can download it and do with it as you wish.

Streamyard on the other hand, is live streaming, and you can go live on all the social media platforms I mentioned on top, live streaming simultaneously on more than one platform at the same time. What will they think of next!

Chapter 17

Email List To Market Your Business/Products

Since 1994 I've built up quite an Email list. I've met people around the globe. I have many friends; I mean face to face friends as well as on social media. I had no idea how many people I personally know. It feels good to have a community of people to support my endeavors, my changes in life. I hope you do this and whenever you can get emails and send newsletters, ads, announcements, and anything to keep in touch with your community. This is important. These are the people that will be there for you and ask if you need help.

I know have almost two thousand contacts on my mobile. Some I have no idea who they are, but I have their phone number and their email. If they are bothered by my email, I will get contacted and unsubscribe them. It's that easy.

Use this tool to ask questions, to ask what they would like to see from you, what advice they have for you. Some of your contacts may have a similar business, ask them questions, ask them if they would help you to understand things clearer, and that you would like their expertise. Almost always people will share their information and help you.

I'd say once a week is good to send an email to your contacts. Once a week, a newsletter, an ad, something, but keep in touch once a week if that works for you, but the key is to be consistent. Your contacts will begin to wait to hear from you and interested to find out what's new in your life. Consistency is the key, and the content should be interesting and new each time.

I have a large family, and well sometimes they are interested in my life and at times, well, they have their burdens. However, I keep them abreast of what I am doing and if any of them can help me, I ask for it.

My sons are geniuses. In high tech and they know the ins and outs of technology. I always ask them for help. Although, really I am very tech savvy, but I still need help in setting things up and the changes that go on every day, it's hard to keep up. I don't know how my sons keep up, I'd be learning about one thing and another thing in the tech world pops up. It is non-stop. The tech world keeps changing and we have to change with it. Technology is great, but there are a lot of negatives about it, too.

With that being said, be careful what you post, what you say, or text, the words can be misconstrued and taken in a twisted way. It can cause a lot of problems or issues. I still believe in the phone call or the in-person contact. It's still the best, you can see and feel the emotions of the contact, you can hear the tone, and see the facial expressions, this is the only heart-felt way that God created from the beginning. Use this as much as possible.

Chapter 18

My Life Today

*I*nitially, this was just an Ebook, I've turned it into a paperback, and I have added more information and chapters. So much has happened to me since I wrote this years ago. I am divorced again, and I am trying to make a living again. Although now my sons are married and I have four grandchildren, I still need to make a living that I am used to. It's not so easy when you are older, but I believe I can do it.

This time in my life, I am still an entrepreneur, that will never change. I have a house that I live in that is now too big for one person. My goal is to sell this one and move into a smaller one story just perfect for me. I am still working as an actress, podcaster and all the things I mentioned earlier. Life has taken me on a different path. I've made some good choices and I've made some bad ones. I ventured out to my dream at ten, Hollywood, Ca, you can read **My Hollywood Daze** for the scoop available on Amazon.

I have made some wise investments in the past regarding real estate, however during the divorce, my ex took half of it. That's what happens. I caught myself in a business marriage and not a love marriage. It was easy for him to not reconcile after thirty years of marriage, he chose a thirty-day relationship with his cleaning lady over me. A cleaning lady who gave him her shoulder to cry on, it was not the first time I felt he had abandoned me. He had many times in our marriage for others. Yet, he still says he loved me, and I broke his heart. Hmmm. The saddest part is that he revealed to me that she does not want him to associate with my sons and his grandchildren. He had to break all ties, with the only family he ever had. That is the saddest of all. A strong man would never allow a woman to control him that way and make him choose the only family he ever had.

I now am closer to my Jesus than I had been in the past. I have learned life is more peaceful and joyuous with him than without him. It's time I learned that. I am diligently writing new books, and have decided to start a publishing company. My books are all about different times in my life and the lessons I have learned a long the way.

I've learned so much in the years and I pray I keep learning. Life is about learning. I love books, and I love people. I am a person who easily forgives when someone hurts, for awhile, but I never hate anyone. I do want to be who God wants me to be. He has made me the BOSS of my life here on earth. He has helped me make better choices for myself and my family. I've dated and I've loved, I am with one man now, it's tenous at times, but I keep hoping God will help us both learn how too communicate better each time we see each other. I pray if this man is not the man that should be in my life, then I know God will send the right man at the right time. I know without a doubt that God will take care of me and provide all my needs.

One thing I do want to stress, no matter what we want to do in life, it's always better if God is in our life, leading our path, the doubts are don'ts. It works!

Chapter 19

Step by Step Guide

1. The dream is necessary.

2. Passion is a must to execute your business success.

3. Create the name you would like for your brand.

4. Go to the County Clerk and to the Secretary of State's office to register and incorporate.

5. Decide if you will make your product or find a manufacturer by googling for companies.

6. Get estimates for production/supply and do what is feasible for you. Start minimally to test the market before you go BIG.

7. Do you need investors? Create a contract for LLC. Start a Limited Liability Company for protection against lawsuits. See attorney for info and to do this if you can't do it yourself. Secretary of State office is where you can file for about $300.

8. Do you want a storefront? If you do, find the location that would be the best demographic for your type of products. Example: You are not going to sell motorcycles in a location where most of the demographic is over seventy years old.

9. Start with small square footage. Don't go too big. Read lease, get attorney to read it if it's too complicated or too much fine print. Beware of fine print.

10. Online business might be your choice. Inventory can be in your basement or a room in your house. Create website for your business. Find a friend who can help you create one. There are

websites that offer web building and help for you to build your own with five pages for a website, your name in url, etc. Many are online, research this on Google as well. One I know of is Homestead.com.

11.   If store or online business is preferred, stock up on inventory minimally to begin.

12.   Create invoices and letterhead on your computer.

13.   You need a computer. Select a printer, copier, scanner, and fax. Most of the time you can get all this from one unit. No need to buy them separately. Purchase office supplies: phone, stapler, filing cabinet, pens and pencils, calendar, tape, etc. If a physical location, decide what equipment you need to start selling your products. Search internet or local fixture stores, Craigslist, etc. for used equipment.

14.   Order business cards. http://www.vistaprint.com offers them FREE—250 free business cards. You can order them free after that as well, and pay only shipping. You will get emails from them always offering a variety of products for free. Check them out as they are great.

15.   Start talking to friends and neighbors about your business and what you are selling. Network yourself and your products. Advertise on the internet. Ask friends to tell their friends about you. Start a business page on Facebook and get networked.

16.   Check the internet and FB pages, see what others are doing, are they successful, if so duplicate with a little modification. Make jewelry, sell beads, bake fudge or cookies and sell them online, fundraisers, etc. Can you make something artsy or craftsy, make it and sell it. Design something, make bling bling t-shirts for women and teens. So many ideas. Just do it!

17.   Start selling and make money.

Chapter 20

Resources

First you have the idea, what you want to create or make, then make a prototype of your idea to see if it will work. Keep this private for now. Then go online and find a non-disclosure form to have all people sign it before you talk about your idea or show your prototype to. Depending on the item, you may be able to license it to a bigger company for a big buyout or royalties. You need your item, product, etc. to be copyrighted, patented, or trademarked. This is where you need a patent or trademark attorney. Usually first visit is free. If you can patent your idea you can do it at this time with attorney or try to do it yourself by going to http://www.uspto.gov. There are companies online that do it for less than $200. Be sure to protect yourself in every way. People and companies will steal your idea if you don't protect yourself asap.

Websites

http://www.homestead.com

http://www.top10bestwebsitehosting.com

http://www.easysiteguide.com

Search http://www.google.com for more ideas.

https://fiverr.com

https://upwork.com

https://streamyard.com

https://zoom.com

Domain Names for Websites

Most popular are these two:

http://www.name.com

http://www.godaddy.com

Social Networks

http://www.facebook.com

http://www.myspace.com

http://www.linkedin.com

http://www.hi5.com

https://instagram.com

https://X.com

http://www.plus.google.com

http://www.orkut.com

http://www.ning.com

http://www.meetup.com

http://www.mylife.com

https://youtube.com

https://zoomus.com

https://streamyard.com

Email Addresses

http://www.google.com/gmail

http://www.yahoo.com

http://www.hotmail.com

Local telephone companies have internet and email addresses. Cable companies have email addresses.

You need an email address in your business name or linked to your website. This helps you communicate with your business partners and vendors. Your local Chamber of Commerce can help you in many ways. Give them a call or a visit. Whatever your need Google search is amazing, and you can find everything you need on the computer.

Remember, if you cannot afford a computer, they are now in libraries and most public places to rent or to pay for by the hour. Be sure not to leave your name, passwords, or email in the history. Make sure the (keep me signed in) is not checked. Others will get into your account and cause you a lot of problems. Keep information to yourself, do not announce publicly any of your passwords.   You are on your way. Let me know if this helped would love to hear from you. I am on Facebook.com. Come and join me. Just Google my name "Nadia Sahari."

About the Author

Nadia Sahari was born in Beirut, Lebanon. She grew up in Dearborn, MI, where she experienced many abuses at home, bullying at school and domestic violence. It took her twenty-five years to get it all into a memoir called BREAKAWAY. She also has written a children's book entitled THE BULLY CAT. Nadia hosts a radio show. Her guests include actors, authors, agents, directors, filmmakers, educators, psychologists, etc. It's all about winning through adversity. She has been given the Award of Courage and the Award of Hope. She is acting and has appeared in several episodes of *Friday Night Lights*, the movie *Bandslam* and is in the upcoming feature film *Corruption.Gov*. Nadia is an activist for the rights of women and children. BREAKAWAY is an inspirational and encouraging read for women, teens, and men too. She has appeared on many national and local television and radio programs, including Great Day SA, San Antonio Living, Smile with B-Mile, EntertainMeTx, Joey Reynolds Show NYC, Michael Dresser Show, Jack Roberts Show, San Antonio Living, and many more. Nadia Sahari donates part of the proceeds to organizations that support women and children. She lists twenty-six of them in her book. Nadia reminds you to break the silence. Get help. You are not alone. There is someone to help you. Do it for yourself and do it for your children. Live your dream. You are worthy. Nadia believes, "If I can do it, anyone can. It is by choice and not by chances that you change your circumstances."

Breakaway: How I Survived Abuse

Nadia Sahari tells the remarkable, true story of her early life. Ms. Sahari was born in Lebanon. ***Breakaway***, her sensational journey through abuse, lifts the veil on her struggle for freedom. Until her early twenties, she was a victim of many abuses, including molestation, repeated beatings, rape, kidnapping, and several attempts on her life. Miraculously she survived. Through it all she clung to her dream to be an actress. She never gave up. Her life story will bring hope and courage to abused women and children everywhere.

The Bully Cat

The Bully Cat, written by best-selling author Nadia Sahari, tells how one cat bullies' other cats and what happens to the bully cat for being just plain mean. Two children, Maia, and Raiden, discover ten stray cats in their yard. The children have fun naming the cats. They love animals but are alarmed when the bully cat comes. The bully cat eats all the food and fights with other cats. What to do? The family finds a creative solution. Children learn about bullying and what they need to do if they are being bullied. No secrets. Beautifully illustrated by artist Olga Rudnitsky and fun to read for all ages.

Nadia Sahari tells how one cat bullies' other cats and what happens to the bully cat for being just plain mean. Two children, Maia, and Raiden, discover ten stray cats in their yard. The children have fun naming the cats. They love animals but are alarmed when the bully cat comes. The bully cat eats all the food and fights with other cats. What to do? The family finds a creative solution. Children learn about bullying and what they need to do if they are being bullied. No secrets. Beautifully illustrated by artist Olga Rudnitsky and fun to read for all ages.

My Hollywood Daze

We all have dreams of being actors, filmmakers, directors, and photographers, etc. Just a goal of going to Hollywood to see the Grauman's Chinese Theatre and spot a movie star walking by. We think of what it could be like to go to Hollywood, live there, attend parties on the red carpet, and maybe meet famous movie stars and take photos with them. Hollywood draws us in with romance, adventure, and mystery through the industry of great movies. The truth is not as it seems, the picture we see is pure fantasy, but what is really behind the image is a cobweb of deceit, evil, drugs, alcohol, prostitution, narcissism, heartbreak, a lot of crime, and homelessness. A world of loneliness, guilt, and turmoil, but many have survived, and in this book, they tell us how they escaped, how they started over in life, asking forgiveness from family, friends, and most of all from God. Letting go and letting God move them into a new experience, new love, and new knowledge and hope. Based on True Hollywood Stories. Names and Events have been changed to protect the innocent. Stories and Characters may appear too good to be true, and they might be true or not.

Be Your Own Boss

A guide that might help anyone who wants to start their own business. This book touches on all kinds of social media, websites, name searches, information of the "How To." What is the passion of the individual, can they start the business and take the risk? The connections, the marketing, the sites, the technology, everything you need to know to help start-ups, and to never give up, keep trying keep doing it. It's your dream, it will happen!

****Dear Reader, I ask with a happy heart that when you read any or all of my books, I have written, please follow me on all my sites, and on Amazon where each book is listed for sale, and write a review of the book you read. Thank you for your support.*
Nadia Sahari

*****You may google my name, and see where I am, what I'm doing, and my new businesses, publications, films, all that I love doing. Please follow me on my social media, let me know you have learned some things from this book. I would love to connect. Check my YouTube channel, see the interviews of successful people.*

All my books are available retail outlets and online.

Available on http://www.amazon.com/;

http://www.barnesandnoble.com/; and at your local bookstores.

Ask them to order it for you if not in stock. Also available on

Kindle and eBooks.

Author's Links

Please join, add or LIKE each of Ms. Sahari's following networks:

http://www.nadiasahari.com
http://www.imdb.me/nadiasahari
http://www.blogtalkradio.com/nadiasahari
http://www.twitter.com/nadiasahari
http://www.facebook.com/nsahari
http://www.myspace.com/nadiasahari
http://www.twitter.com/nadiasaharishow
http://www.linkedin.com/nadiasahari
http://www.nadiasahari.blogspot.com
https://www.instagram.com/nadiasahariofficial
https:www.facebook.com/nadiasahariauthor
https:www.youtube.com/@nadiasahari

https://www.pinterest.com/nadiasahari
https://www.goodreads.com/author/show/2848020.Nadia_Sahari

Videos

http://www.youtube.com/watch?v=SfSpVkvGL4Q
http://www.youtube.com/watch?v=L0jXNUo09JU
http://www.youtube.com/watch?v=GKILF5G6x7I
http://www.youtube.com/watch?v=AhRH1klSXak
http://www.youtube.com/watch?v=-
GuuSQRb8og&feature=related
http://www.youtube.com/watch?v=SD0xo71ZqFg&feature=youtu
be_gdata

http://www.amazon.com/s/ref=nb_sb_noss?url=search-
alias%3Dstripbooks&field-
keywords=the+bully+cat+by+nadia+sahari&x=19&y=18

http://www.amazon.com/Breakaway-How-I-Survived-
Abuse/dp/0982041306/ref=sr_1_1?s=books&ie=UTF8&qid=1301
254537&sr=1-1

**Thank you from my heart, for supporting me, reading, and
viewing my work. God bless you all, and God bless America
and the whole world.**

***One final message: The most Important thing in our lives we
need to do, is be certain and be sure we have faith in God, and his
Son Jesus, the Holy Spirit, all 3 are one. He is our God, who
created us, who allows us to choose our lives. We all have a
destiny. If you don't have a personal relationship with God, please
read Romans Road, available on: https://www.got questions.org.
And on your mobile, there is a great App called 'Holy Bible"
created by YouVersion. This App has videos, all Bibles
translations, Torah, and many courses and more than any other

App. Its FREE! It's wonderful! And it's Free, The Chosen Seasons 1-3 are on there for FREE. Get this App. It's a fabulous source to research and learn all about God.